With warm friendly thoughts.

Fondly,
Cynthia Holt Cummings

To Grandma Laura
from
Andy & Anne

Christmas '93

Christmas Dreams

Christmas is a dream we trace
With each new snowflake on our face.

The spirit of Christmas
Is heard in a prayer,
From the little child
Who is kneeling there.

When you teach a child to pray
You give him love for each new day.

This little book contains much love
And in between the lines—
I hope you too will all recall
Some happy Christmas times.

Christmas Dreams

Poems by Cynthia Holt Cummings

Illustrated by Fritz Henning

Holt Peterson Press
Birmingham, Michigan

Other illustrated (black & white) books of poetry and verse by Cynthia Holt Cummings published by Holt Peterson Press, Inc., Box 940, Birmingham, MI 48012. Author narration on audio cassettes also available.

Books in which selected Christmas poems in this volume were originally published:

> Christmas Ribbons
> Christmas Memories
> Christmas Love
> Christmas Wishes
> Christmas Treasures

Christmas teddy bear stories in verse:

> Christmas Surprise
> Christmas Joy
> Christmas Spirit

Christmas Dreams

Collection of previously published
Christmas verse by Cynthia Holt Cummings.
Illustrated by Fritz Henning.

Printed in The United States of America.
First printing, September, 1992.

ISBN 1-881811-09-3

**For my husband
of forty-five years**

Into the world I lifted a pen,
And the following poems were written then.

Angels

Angels carol this winter night
While children down below
Look up to see the star so bright
Reflecting Christmas in the snow.

What Christmas Is

Christmas is touching;
Looking for love in the children's eyes;
Trimming a tree with holly and lights.
Placing a star up high--
Wrapping each gift with special care.
Bowing your head,
And saying a prayer.

Echo

The trumpet sounds to praise God's name,
And the echo is heard in a candle's flame.

Christmas Prayer

Christmases come,
Christmases go,
With the green fir trees
And the cold white snow.
Because a child is walking there,
Peace for all
Is our Christmas prayer.

Christmas for Buff and Roger

This year a little miracle
Will see your Christmas tree.
A little lad who's not quite one
Will crawl around your knee.

The tree will have a special glow
To welcome in the day.
Every present tied with bow
Will soon be torn away.

On the floor his little hands
Will reach for one and all,
The building blocks, the windup toy,
The teddy and the ball.

Together you will play
With contentment in your heart,
For how could any Christmas day
Have a better start?

Oh count your blessings one by one
Be thankful once again,
For Him who came so long ago
To bring peace on earth-good will to men.

David Michael's First Christmas

Dear David. . . . it's Christmas
That special time each year
When hearts are filled with happiness
And greetings of good cheer;
And all the little children
Close their eyes in sleep
Awaiting Christmas morning
For secrets stockings keep.

Candy canes and jumping jacks,
Little black trains that run on tracks,
A bright red sled and spinning tops,
Boxes filled with candy drops,
Picture books with nursery rhymes,
Music boxes filled with chimes,
Popcorn balls and apples red,
A teddy bear, a dolly's bed,
Little toy soldiers straight and tall,
A bag of blocks, a bright blue ball.

It's Christmas, David . . . .
A time for merry laughter
A knock upon the door.
A little lad like you
Plays with toys on the floor.

A time to love each other
To say a little prayer,
To reach with tighter handclasp
For the treasures that we share.

A time to be so thankful
For the friends we hold so dear.
Oh, David . . . . it's so special
When Christmas comes each year.

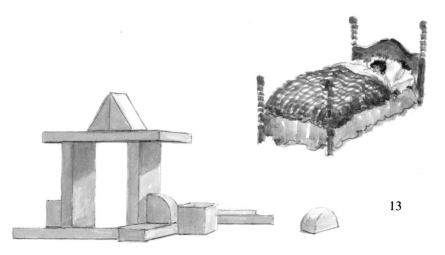

A Prayer for Peace and Love

Green fir tree
With Christmas light
Reach out to all
The world tonight
And with the star
So high above
Spread the prayer
For peace and love.

Remembering

A Christmas carol
Soon will ring
With everyone
Remembering.

It's such a simple thing,
Remembering—

Faith, Joy and Love

If love is in the stocking,
And joy is on the tree,
If faith is in the glowing star,
Then friendship is the key
To blessings in the coming year,
With faith and joy and love quite near.

For The Children

May Christmas peace
Fill all the land
With children walking
Hand in hand
And may the joy
Of Christmas light
Sparkle in their eyes
Tonight.

Peace

Peace is such a precious thing
So thankful we should be
To gather with our family
Around the Christmas tree.

Whenever I see a green fir tree
Christmas comes again to me.

What Christmas Is All About

One little light blinks on and off,
One little bell rings out,
One little hand holds onto yours,
And you know what Christmas is all about.

Christmas Is

Christmas is a drift of snow,
One red candle all aglow,
A tree with star placed high above,
A ribboned present tied with love.

Gather love on Christmas day
And let your heart give it away.

Christmas Love

It's Christmas
And the snow and I,
Walk hand and hand,
Beneath the sky.
I look above,
The star so bright,
Gives Christmas love
Again tonight.
Oh thank you God,
Once more I pray,
For Christmas love,
To fill my day.

Favorite Treasure

In the chest
Were all her treasures
Summer days had been such fun.
Tiny stones and soft bird feathers
She had saved them one by one.
Now at Christmastime once more,
She opened up the chest
And gave her favorite treasure
To the one she loved the best.

17

Christmas Ribbons

Save your Christmas ribbons
To tie in Julie's hair
A blue one for the sky above
And red for roses fair
Green will tell of springtime
With robins on the wing
And yellow is the color
For all the songs they sing.
Save your Christmas ribbons
To tie in Julie's hair
Silver is for laughter
And all the dreams you share
Ribbons are like flowers
That in a garden grow
Their colors make a rainbow
Fashion diamonds in the snow.
Gold is for the treasured jewel
But none can 'ere compare
With a little girl like Julie
Wearing Christmas ribbons in her hair.

Christmas Gift

This Christmas card, our gift to you,
Is brightly tied with ribbons red,
Inside we packed, the whole year through.
Some words of kindness that we'd said.

And in the songs we heard each day
That made our hearts feel light,
We put a note of each new one
In to the corners tight.

Then in the middle of the box
We found some space to spare;
And this we filled with happiness,
That each of you might share.

And so once more at Christmas time,
When homes are bright and gay,
We wrap our Christmas Gift to you
And send it on its way.

A Difficult Choice

A little girl's face pressed against the pane
Of the big store window that day.
Inside, once again, she saw the dolls
All in their bright array.
Oh, Santa, please bring me the one in red,
With her little fur muff of white,
She's just the right size for my dolly's bed
And I'll tuck her in at night.
Then suddenly the little girl
Saw the doll with real curly hair,
And she thought for just a moment
Of her tiny rocking chair.
'Twould be such fun to have a doll
With hair so soft and brown,
And she could sit in her little chair,
And rock her to sleep so sound.
But then far in the corner
Was a doll in snowy white,
Dressed as a bride for a wedding,
All on a Christmas night.
Oh, the little girl was puzzled,
They were all so sweet and nice,
Especially the one wearing silver skates
To glide across the ice.
And there was a doll in a dance frock
Of the prettiest shade of blue,
Right next to the one in baby clothes
With a tag marked "Sister Sue".
'Twas difficult for the little girl
To choose for her very own,
The doll that Santa would bring Christmas eve
To live in her world at home.

Christmas Music

I love the music for Christmas day,
Carols sung in the same old way,
Voices of old and those so young,
Christmas carols from every tongue.

Oh, for the music of Christmas day,
Bringing the greatest joy
To every tiny little girl,
To every growing boy.

Music soft and sweet and clear,
Echoing from the voices here,
Filling air with music bright,
Music sung on a Christmas night.

Christmas Glow

A cane, a doll, but that's not all;
There's love beneath the tree.

A book, a pen, now look again,
And in the star you'll see

The gold, the light that shines so bright,
That all the world may know

The joy, the peace that gives each face
That special Christmas glow.

Christmas Star

Oh the brightness of the leaf
When Autumn's all aglow
That thoughts could venture forth
To forests white with snow.

Above it all a brilliant star
To tell us all once more
The glory of the Christ child
As in Christmases before.

As though the yellow leaf
Reached up so high above
To give the star its glory
And fill the world with love.

God's Christmas Gift

With faith in your dream
You know the reason why
God's Christmas gift
Was a star in the sky.

A Mother's Christmas Prayer

In the twilight of the evening, sat a mother,
    hair of gray.
Rocking slowly in her chair, thinking thoughts
    of Christmas day.
Now the house, so very quiet on this early
    Christmas eve,
Soon would fill with happy laughter, children
    coming home would weave.
All year long, how she had waited for her
    children now to see
Once again in home of childhood gathered closely
    round the tree.
In the window, burning brightly, stood the yellow
    candles fair,
Sending out their Christmas message of a mother's
    silent prayer.
Please, Lord, make their trip a safe one, so that
    I may see once more
Happy faces of my children coming in my white
    front door.
Let me tell them once again of the glowing light
    that night,
As shepherds watching flocks looked up and saw
    the star so bright.

The Beauty of Christmas

I looked out my window in the darkness of night,
Saw the tree all aglow with its Christmas light,
Spreading cheer for the Christmas that soon would come,
With peace here on earth to everyone.

And there, on the door of my neighbor,
Hung a wreath circled in light,
Like a halo of friendliness spoken,
For the coming of Christmas night.

The light-falling snow recovered the old,
With a brilliance of sparkling white,
And the sky overhead made the stars hidden bed,
All safely tucked in for the night.

And there on each roof was a blanket
Of downy new-fallen snow,
That covered the houses, with children
Sleeping ever so soundly below.

And the mother and dad before fireplace
Talked of a Christmas bright,
And the glow in the room was felt by both,
Of the coming of Christmas night.

I stood and looked at the beauty
That greeted my eyes in the night,
From a tree and a wreath lit with brilliance,
Reflecting their Christmas light.

Christmas Is For

Christmas is for little boys
Toys beneath the tree
Brightly tied with ribbons
Tiny fingers hold the key.

Christmas is for little girls
With ribbons in their hair
Oh to see their eyes light up
As they descend the stair.

Christmas is for older folk
With wrinkles on their brow
Christmas is forever
Christmas is for now.

The Little Clown

He walked and he hopped
And he bowed way down
Such was the dance
Of the little clown.

He opened his eyes
And then closed them tight
The light of the star
Was glowing so bright.

He raised his hands
To touch the tree
And he thought of the splendor
The world would see.

He winked and he blinked
And he counted the toys
Marked with bright tags
For the girls and the boys.

Around and around
The tree he went
The minutes, the hours
Were quickly spent.

The clock was chiming
In the hall
And Christmas was ready
For one and all.

Silhouette

Snowflakes slowly floating from the dense gray sky
Built drifts of downy white piled ever so high.
And as the tiny snowflakes all day kept falling.
Autumn left by the back door and winter came calling.
The valley was winter in white once more.
As I looked at its beauty from my own front door.
The fir trees beckoned with new weighted snow
That painted their branches now hanging so low.
Bright diamonds sparkled on the white-blanketed ground,
As the wind danced the snowflakes around and around;
The little birds took cover from the light falling snow
In the candy-tufted bushes nestled in a row.
Soon the daylight hours slipped into night,
And winter became a silhouette all in black and white.

Bright Red Bow

I'm giving love this Christmas
To all the friends I know
I'm wrapping it with laughter
Tied with a bright red bow.

The Magic of Christmas

I'm counting the days until Christmas,
I'm watching the skies fall down
With snowflakes that come so gently
To cover the earth of brown.

I'm wrapping the gifts for Christmas
With love and joy in my heart
And I'm ending the year with magic
To give the new year a start.

The trees that are tall and stately
In their winter coats of green
Will soon wear the colors of Christmas
Become part of the Christmas scene.

Lights will be blinking,
Bells will be ringing,
Voices will echo with song,
Oh for the magic of Christmas
To last the whole year long.

A Christmas Greeting

I've thought about Christmas,
The star and the tree;
The lights in the windows for all to see.
The red ribboned bows on presents galore,
The toys on the counter in many a store.

I've thought about Christmas
Both morning and night,
I've searched for a message
That would be just right.
I've thought about wishes
And greetings we send
As Christmas approaches
At each year's end.

And my heart over-flowed
With thoughts of love
As I thought of the Savior
And the star above--
And so to each friend
Both near and far
We send you our love
In the shape of a star.

The Christmas Elf

I saw him peeking through the door,
You know the Christmas elf—
He thought it was his duty
To trim the tree himself.

He wore a little suit of red,
His hair was snowy white,
And tiny little buttons
Held his shoes on tight.

He seemed to be so merry
For one so very small—
I wondered could he ever
Trim a tree so tall?

He circled round and round the tree
So quickly one could hardly see
The little buttons on his shoes,
But on each turn he'd stop to choose
A tiny bell, a candy cane,
And circle all around again.

Little ropes of tinsel,
Little wreaths with bows
Quickly left their places
And where do you suppose?

I watched with all my wonder
A sight my eyes could see
How a little elf at Christmas
Trimmed the tree for me.

The star it shone so brightly
Through the windowpane,
I hope that when it's Christmas
The elf will come again!

The Light of Love

Decorate this little tree
With love and joy and then—
Give once again the treasured gift
Of peace on earth, good will to men.
Sit back and watch the branches glow
With light that only LOVE can show.

Christmas Joy

This Christmas may we wish you all,
Some joys that come both large and small.
Warm sunshine on a summer day,
The children's laughter while at play.
A rainbow that a sunset makes,
And courage that a new deed takes.
The autumn leaves with colors bright,
A star-filled sky on a winter's night.
The greetings from a new found friend,
A peaceful sleep at daytime's end.
Keep all the joys we send your way,
This is our Christmas wish today.

Ballerina

Tiny ballerina snowflake,
Under spotlight moon so bright,
Whistling wind your magic music,
Winter's stage you dance tonight.

Be Thankful

Walk slowly thru the snow this year
Feel the cold breeze touch your cheek
Greet neighbor with a friendly hand
Listen to the children speak.

Walk slowly thru the snow this year
Beneath a starlit sky
Be thankful for your happiness
As Christmas passes by.

One Little Hand Took Hold of Mine

One little hand took hold of mine,
"Come see the snow, it's Christmastime!"
Oh no not yet, I soon replied.
Not until each present is wrapped and tied.
And the tree is trimmed with colored lights.
And the star on top is glowing bright.

One little hand took hold of mine.
"Come see the snow, it's Christmastime!"
Oh no not yet, I answered again,
First come the shepherds and the three wisemen—
And the little stable will be dimly lit
Where Joseph and Mary will quietly sit
To watch over the babe with the star so bright.
To welcome in the holy night.

40

One little hand took hold of mine,
"Come see the snow, it's Christmastime!"
At last the day was really here:
The tree was trimmed
And the family near—
And the music of voices filled the air
With the spirit of Christmas beyond compare.

One little hand took hold of mine,
"Come see the snow, it's Christmastime!"

The Candy Cane Ballet

On a stage of snow under starlit glow,
The candy canes began to dance;
And the music of the whistling wind
Could be heard thru every branch
Of all the trees in the forest there
Standing so straight and tall,
Watching the candy cane ballet
As Christmas came to call.

The squirrels and the rabbits
Were as quiet as could be,
For a candy cane ballet
Was a special sight to see.
Louder and louder the whistling wind
Whistled thru the trees,
Faster and faster the dancers spun
Bowing to their knees.

Suddenly the candy canes became so
        very still,
As the morning sun was rising
Over the snow-capped hill.
The whistling wind became quiet,
And the rabbits scampered away,
And the squirrels followed quickly
For this was Christmas day.

The children say
In the town that day
The people all were talking,
About lacey patterns in the snow
They had seen when they were walking.

The Children's Room

This is the room
Where the children play
They're serving tea
To the bears today

The music boxes
Are all wound up
And the teddy bears listen
As they drink from the cup

The dolls in their dresses
Of pink and blue
Are learning a dance
That is very new

The doll in the cradle
Rocks to and fro
To the lullaby music
Bears only know

They are playing games
Of chance today
And the prize is a smile
They give away

This is the room
Where the children play
And just for awhile
I'm a child today.

A Childhood Dream

Memories come and memories go
In candlelight and falling snow;
Blinking lights on every tree
Reflect a childhood dream to me.

The first new sled beneath the tree—
Adventure for a child of three.
Up and down the hill I'd go
To pull the tiny sled in snow.
My laughter echoed in the air—
Childhood dreams were everywhere.
Oh to be a child once more,
To set the spirit free;
To travel back to winterland
When I was only three.
To see the hills with childhood eyes,
To feel the falling snow;
To build a childhood dream once more
How quickly I would go.

Memories come and memories go
In candlelight and falling snow.
Blinking lights on every tree
Reflect a childhood dream to me.

How Much Love

How much more love
        could a Christmas card hold,
Than when written by the hand
        of a 3-year old?

Memories

The tree is new with branches green;
It stands so straight and tall.
I see the children once again
When they were very small.

I'm hanging Christmas ornaments
To decorate the tree.
In fading colors once so bright
I'm hanging memory.

The little angel still has wings
With a halo made of gold.
The china bell no longer rings
But in it's silence holds,
The memories I now recall
When all the children were so small,
And laughter echoed in the hall.

Christmas Colors

Grandchildren legs are stretched on
        the floor;
Hands are coloring books once more.
Green for the tree and gold for the star;
Thoughts of Christmas are not very far.
Santa's suit is a bright, bright red;
His boots are shiny black.
All of this in a coloring book,
Bringing a Christmas back.

Love Song

I'm writing a love song for Christmas
As I look at the beautiful tree.
I'm remembering scenes from
    my childhood
With the love of my family.

I'm stringing ropes of red cranberries
To hang 'neath the star of gold.
Oh the wonderful memories of childhood
A love song for Christmas can hold.

I can hear the chime of the church bells
Echoing over the hill.
I can see Santa's sleigh on its journey
With so many stockings to fill.

And as candles glowed in each window
And the snowflakes came falling down—
We would sing Christmas carols to
    the shut-ins
In that little countrytown.

The laughter and love in my childhood
That all of this could be mine—
To share in a love song for Christmas
With others this Christmastime.

The Gold Band

She held the ribbons in her hand
Of red and green and blue,
She looked beneath the tree and saw
The presents that were new.

The little china figurine
The pretty light blue vase,
Reminded her of years gone by
Spent in a different place.

The sun was setting in the west
Upon a field of snow,
And once again she knew so well
That Christmas day must go.

Among the colored ribbons
She saw the plain gold band,
And realized the love she had
Was held there in her hand.

The Toys' Celebration

Rocking and rocking, the little horse
Was waiting for Christmas morn;
Rocking, rocking, he waited and listened
For the sound of the soldier's horn.
The jack-in-the-box raised his head,
We must hurry before they wake;
And the little horse just rocked and rocked
Then gave his tail a shake.

The little toy soldier blew his horn
And the notes came loud and clear;
The dolls were ready to take their bows
As the teddy bear gave a cheer.
The little train just puffed and puffed
Around the track on the floor,
And the lion began to roll about
Then gave a mighty roar.

On the top of the tree the little Star
Was as happy as could be,
Never before had there been such a sight
Beneath the Christmas tree

48

The music box began to play
And the dolls all clapped their hands,
And the rocking horse just rocked and rocked
To the rhythm of the band.

The toylike celebration
Was a special sight to see,
And the little star just glowed and glowed
At the top of the Christmas tree.

The rocking horse became very still
And he turned his head to hear;
I hear a noise, be quiet, be quiet,
The children will soon be near.
The music box was all run down
And the lion was fast asleep,
And everyone was back in place
With the secrets they would keep.
Oh look—oh look, the children cried,
What a beautiful sight to see;
And the only one that was still awake
Was the star on the Christmas tree.

Paper Chains

Children fashion paper chains to
    decorate the tree,
And in the colored circles, childhood
    dreams come back to me.
Paper chains of red and green I
    made so long ago,
When green trees grew upon the hill
    in New England fields of snow.
A mother's dream of childhood
    doesn't seem so very far,
When the yellow one is chosen to
    match the glowing star.
Colored circles capture LOVE as
    they're hung upon the tree,
And all the dreams of childhood
    come quickly back to me.

I Bring You Love

I bring you love, she said to me,
To put beneath the Christmas tree.
I nurtured it the whole year long
With notes I heard from each bird's song.
And when a child would smile at me
I gathered love for the family.
Strange how love can grow and grow
To mingle with a flake of snow.
The wrapping was not hard to find;
I could not pick just any kind.
I searched my heart, and with a kiss,
It took one hug for all of this.
I place it in your tender care,
To put beneath the tree right there.
While up above the star so bright,
Received her love on Christmas night.

The Walking Doll

The walking doll was looking up,
Looking up to see—
The beautiful star—the beautiful star
At the top of the Christmas tree.

The little toy soldier opened his eyes
Then stood up straight and tall.
He turned his head and then he saw
The lovely walking doll.
Now the walking doll had never seen
A soldier in red and blue.
She quickly turned her head away
Not knowing what to do.

Just take my hand the soldier said,
No reason to be afraid.
The star will guide us with its light,
That's why stars were made.

The music box began to play
As the doll took the soldier's hand;
And that is the way the star will say
The Christmas ball began.
The ornaments were swaying
And the bells began to chime.

The presents danced beneath the tree
They were having a merry time.
Dancing and dancing around the tree,
The soldier in red and blue,
Held in his arms a walking doll
Who knew her love would be true.
The beautiful star at the top of the tree
Looked down on the pair below;
Giving its blessing to each of them
With its Christmas starlit glow.

As Christmases would come and go
The soldier in blue and red,
Would look at the lovely walking doll
With the star high overhead.
And the walking doll would remember
A Christmas long ago,
Standing beside a Christmas tree
Under the starlit glow;
When a soldier had said
Just take my hand,
No reason to be afraid.
The star will guide us with its light,
That's why stars were made.

Grandchildren

Where are the children?
Where have they gone?
I once heard their laughter,
I once heard their song.

There are toys in the attic,
Toys in the hall,
Toys in big boxes,
For children so small.

Bring me the dolls.
Wind up the train.
They're coming home
With children again.

Find the toy soldier,
Once shiny and new.
Bring me the tea set
Of china so blue.

I'll polish the table.
I'll place every chair,
With joy in my heart,
With the children there.

Where are the children?
Where have they gone?
Once more I'll hear laughter,
Once more I'll hear song.

Mother's Gifts

In her lap a piece of linen
With an intricate design;
I would often see my mother
Making gifts for Christmastime.

From the strands of colored floss
She could make the flowers bloom;
She was growing summer's garden
Just to warm a winter room.

Threading needles by the hour
With each stitch a bit of love;
She gave roses in December
When the star was high above.

How Much I Love You

I've done many things for Christmas;
I've tied each present with bow,
But there's one other thing
I wanted to tell you,
How much I love you,
But I think you know.

Christmas Wishes

I saw a jolly Santa sitting in a chair.
And on his lap a tiny lad ran fingers through his hair.
Please Santa will you bring
A little doll for sister Sue
And Mom would like a brand new ring
With stone of sapphire blue.

Now Dad would like an easy chair,
A place to sit when day is done:
And Santa please bring me
A little train to run.

I know your sleigh will be so full
When Christmas rolls round,
But if there's just a little space,
Bring smiles to wear on every face.

Christmas Thoughts

(Written in North Africa—1943)

We are far away from you all tonight
In this land across the sea,
No Christmas lights to brighten our way.
As there are on your Christmas tree.
But shining high above us
Are the moon and the stars spreading light,
Sent by God's hand to comfort and guide us
On this, our Christmas night.

We know that you all may miss us,
But we hope and solemnly pray
That when Christmas time rolls round again
We will be home with you—home to stay.
So keep Christmas the same as you have before,
With laughter and merriment bright,
For even though a chair may be vacant,
We are with you there tonight.

Christmas Stocking

Between the age of three and four
I hung a stocking Mother wore . . . .
No fancy trim, just pinned to the chair
To be ready and waiting for Santa there.
On Christmas morn I'd quickly look
To find a brand new coloring book . . . .
A pencil box with tiny key
Would fill the stocking to the knee.
Walnuts and an orange round
Were safely tucked below . . . .
And when I stretched my hand way down
Pennies filled the toe.

The Friendly Hand

This Christmas may there friendly, be—
A neighbor's hand stretched out to me.
If only in a bright porch light
That shows the shape of trees at night;
Or when the window shade is drawn
Upwards to greet the sun that morn;
To let me know that someone's there
Across the road which we both share.
The friendly gesture showing why
The Star that night is in the sky.

Christmas Window

Give me a Christmas window
So I will be able to see
The flame of a bright red candle
And the star on the top of the tree.

Give me a Christmas window
Where I may look at the star
And remember the wise men traveling
To Bethlehem ever so far.

Give me a Christmas window
Where friends may look as they pass
And feel the love of Christmas
Reaching out through the panes of glass.

Patch of Blue

The bluejay flying by,
Like a patch of blue
Torn from the sky.

Hurry, Hurry, Hurry

Hurry, hurry, hurry
Christmas will soon be here
But stop awhile
Enjoy the smile
Of a child that's very near.

Hurry, hurry, hurry
It's better to go slow
Enjoy the candle
And the tree
With peaceful light aglow.

Hurry, hurry, hurry
So many things to do
Hesitate, meditate
Your strength you will renew.

Hurry, hurry, hurry
Christmas day is here
Take time to say I love you
Before the bright new year.

Love for Little Children

It's our love for little children
That keeps Christmas all year long.
As we listen to their laughter,
We can make a Christmas song.
As we take their hands and lead them,
All the days throughout the year,
We can show them that we love them,
And keep their love quite near.

Walk with Me

Walk with me this Christmas;
See the lights aglow,
Reflecting Christmas greetings
In the winter snow.
Peace and love are all around;
There's music in the air,
Voices singing carols, echo everywhere.
Walk with me this Christmas;
See the glowing star,
Sending out its message
To friends both near and far.
Be thankful in your heart again
For peace on earth,
Good will to men.

Christmas Is

Christmas is a present
Tied with red bow
A bright glowing star
A field white with snow.
A tree that is green,
Trimmed with tinsel and gold,
Christmas is love,
For a stocking to hold.

Christmas Jewel

She wears a jewel with majesty
The evergreen—the Christmas tree
The star of gold on top you'll see
Look up—look up—it says to me
A crown of hope and faith and love
Speaks to all from high above
A jewel that lasts through all the years
Still sparkles on with faith through tears
And as each Christmas time draws near
To welcome in another year
Look up—look up—take time to see
The beautiful jewel at the top of the tree.

Christmas Greetings

We receive your Christmas greetings
And wonder if you know
The joy and friendship
That they bring
When earth is white with snow.
Like candles on a table
Lit with a yellow flame
Your greetings carry friendship
To our Christmas hearts again.
And so we treasure greetings
We can't buy within a store
Your love is ours to cherish
For just one Christmas more.

Christmas Light

The night was so cold
But the little star
Was as bright
As a star could be.
It looked below
On the mountains
And stretched its light
To the sea.
It made the church steeple glisten
In every country town
In the cold of the night
The Christmas light
Came gently shining down.

Chiming

I hear them ringing in the hills
And in the valley too.
Church bells chiming carols
Oh so old, but oh so new.
Telling of the holy birthday
Of a child born long ago.
Church bells chiming, chiming, chiming,
All across the winter snow.

Many Things

I love Christmas for many things
Trees, candles, angel wings.
Stars in the heavens,
Snow covered hills,
Little toy trains,
Dolls in their frills.

I love Christmas, ribbons of gold,
Familiar carols, so very old.
Sweet candy canes, bright red sleds,
Little ones tucked snug in their beds.

I love Christmas, but most of all
I look forward to a neighbor's call.
A friendly chat, a cup of tea
Love in the home means Christmas to me.

I Tie My Love With Ribbons

In the glow of Christmas candles
And the stars that shine above,
I bring you season's greetings
With my ribboned gift of love.
In the joyous sound of voices
Singing carols in the snow,
I take your hand and tell you
Of my love that seems to grow.
With Christmas years behind us
And Christmas years ahead,
I tie my love with ribbons
In the shade of Christmas red.

When Christmas Comes Each Year

It's the joy of children
The warmth of love
The many blessings
Beneath the star above
The many friends we know
The neighbors living near
That makes our lives so special
When Christmas comes each year.

Jessica

You tell Jessica a story sitting in your lap.
You tuck her in for her afternoon nap,
You pick up her toys, you comb Jessica's hair,
These are the moments you two will share.

You take Jessica out for a morning walk.
You listen carefully to Jessica talk,
You hear birds sing, you pick springtime flowers,
Your days are filled with happy hours.

You smile and you laugh when you're together,
No matter the time or what kind of weather,
You go to her teaparties under the tree,
She builds in her sandbox a castle to see.

Wearing pretty dresses with a sparkle in her eyes
She will always give you a bright surprise,
From down below she looks up at you
With a little girl expression that is always new.

She will clap her hands and wave good by,
Shake her head and give a big sigh,
She will tug at your skirt and hide her face,
She knows you'll reach down with a mother's embrace.

The years will go by so very fast,
So make every moment with Jessica last,
And when she is grown you'll remember so well
When Jessica climbed on your lap for a story to tell.

Sleep Little One

Sleep little one
Under the star
I'll watch over you
I won't be far.
Angels will sing
Their carols tonight
Under the star
Glowing so bright.
Sleep little one
Under the star
I'll watch over you
I won't be far.
Angel voices
In carols sing
A birthday greeting
To the newborn king.
Sleep little one
Under the star
I'll watch over you
I won't be far.

What Will I Give Her?

What will I give her for Christmas . . .
Long stem roses of brightest red
Or maybe a silver chain instead?
A white fur muff to warm her hands
Or books with stories of far off lands?
A music box that's filled with song
To show my love the whole day long?
What will I give her for Christmas . . .
I ask it over and over again
When I know that the answer
Is always the same,
I'll give her my heart to mend.

70

Christmas Gift

A chain of love I'll give to you
With trinkets old and trinkets new.
Some are silver—some are gold
But tucked there in between,
Are bits of tin and shiny brass
And pieces made of crystal glass.
For life holds joys and sorrows too
As years go quickly by;
Each helps to make love stronger
Reasons never tell us why.
Joy and sorrow are all a part
To make love stronger in our heart.
A chain of love I'll give to you
With trinkets old and trinkets new.

Remembering

Peace be with you
This coming year;
As seasons change
Give way to spring,
Take time for a little
Remembering;
For friends you met
Along your way
Who helped to brighten
Up a day;
For little things
That mean so much,
A child's smile,
A loved one's touch.
Peace be with you
This coming year
Remembering things
You hold so dear.

God's Mailbox

Dear Daddy;

It's Christmas and time to write
My own special letter to you tonight.
On the floor neatly placed under the tree
Are the pretty wrapped gifts for all to see,
And on the very tip top—oh up so far—
I've pinned a brightly gold-lit star.
The first letter I wrote when I was four
And Santa had brought me the doll from his store;
That was the year just before Christmas day
You told Mommy and me you were going away.
War had darkened the big land across the sea
And you went to help to keep our home free.
We missed you so Daddy—my Mommy and me,
And we waited and waited as each Christmas tree
Was trimmed with the lights so pretty and bright,
And your chair remained vacant each Christmas night.
Then the Christmas when I was finally eight—
Oh Daddy it was getting so very late—
And when you hadn't returned from the land so far
'Twas then Mommy told me about the gold star
That God had placed in his heaven so blue,
The star for my Daddy—it was just for you.

As each Christmas passes since I was four,
I sit down and write your letter once more,
And before I close my eyes in sleep that night
I drop it in God's mailbox, and soon it's in flight.

It reaches your star, and you read it right then,
And learn of the things that have happened since when
You left us that day so long, long ago
When the brown earth was covered with new winter snow.

The sweaters, so pretty when I was eleven,
Were gold for your star and blue for your heaven,
And the star cast its glow in the room that night
And reached out to touch your star so bright.
Tonight, Daddy, they tell me I'm a junior miss
And this letter I'll seal with a special kiss,
Add a dash of the perfume so sweet-scented I wear
And enclose a small lock of my brown curly hair.
In the closet my treasures, the ball and the top,
And the little store doll that Santa brought,
And on my dresser I plainly see
The picture of Mommy, my Daddy and me.
Oh the chair may be vacant, my Daddy, tonight,
But up in God's heaven, shining so bright,
Is the big gold star that will always last,
No matter the years that slip quickly past.
And in those years I'll always write
The letter for God's mailbox on Christmas night.
And as the sun sinks in the sky so blue,
Giving way to dark night once more anew,
I'll look in God's heaven and see shining bright,
The gold star God gave you one Christmas night.

Christmas Carol

I can hear you scampering little mouse
High in the attic of this old house.
What are you looking for?
Is it still there?
The tiny toy soldier,
The old rocking chair,
Is it the tinsel to trim the tree?
Or cards from old friends
In a trunk with a key?
The train is still packed,
The drum doesn't beat,
And I know little mouse
There is nothing to eat.
The attic door opened,
With the chime of a bell;
Santa had come
With your secret to tell.
As he opened his pack,
The little bell chime
Told me again,
It was Christmastime.

So when it is Christmas,
I listen once more
For your scampering feet
On the old attic floor.
And soon I can hear,
I know it so well,
Your own Christmas carol,
The chime of a bell.

I Wonder

I wonder—said the little boy
What makes God's sky so blue?
How can the grass be freshly damp
With early morning dew?
What makes the trees so big and strong
To hold my flying swing?
Why God is really able to do most everything.
He paints the leaves with colors bright
When autumn comes each year,
He places high the Christmas star
To bring the Christchild near.
I wonder—said the little boy
What makes God's sky so blue?
And then he saw the answer
When the morning sun broke thru.

No Greater Treasure

No greater treasure
Could be mine,
Than someone's love
At Christmas time.

Toy Soldier

Toy soldier, take care of the children tonight,
Keep the star of peace glowing so bright.

Christmas Lullaby

Cozy and warm from the winter snow.
She remembers the star with its Christmas glow.
She thinks of the days and year ahead.
As she tucks the children into bed.

I'll give them love and teach them to pray,
I'll show them how to give smiles away.
I'll help them build castles in the sand,
And teach them to give a helping hand.
I'll let them know what it is to share,
So someone will know that they really care.
I'll help them grow in the kindly way,
And give them some happiness every day.

This is the lullaby she sings tonight,
With the star high overhead.
This is her Christmas lullaby,
As she tucks the children into bed.

Children's Laughter

Music is the children's laughter
Filling up the room.
Echoes come forever after,
Do not let it end too soon.
Let your soul fill up with music,
Gather love inside your heart,
For the day that's in the future,
When children's laughter will depart.

Give Love Once Again

Send a greeting this year
To someone who's old,
Someone with memories
Of green and of gold.
How many times
She tied ribbons of red,
Hustled around
To tuck children in bed.
Filled the stockings
With gifts of love,
Gave thanks for her blessings
To the star above.
Send a greeting this year
To someone who's old.
Give love once again
For her heart to hold.

What Is It?

Is it the sparkle on the tree,
The green wreath on the door,
The present tied with ribbon red,
Or is it something more?
The cheery greeting when we meet
A friend along our way,
The crunch of snow beneath our feet,
The children in their play?
We ask ourselves,
What is it?
But in the end we know
It's our love for one another
That makes Christmas spirit glow.

Cheer

Hands folded in prayer
Christmas is there, and
When I speak a word of cheer
I've kept Christmas through the year.

Jack Frost

By the light of a star he paints at night
In winter cold when the earth is white.
Delicate lace on the window pane
While Christmas is filling the world again.
Icicle brushes in his sack
A snowflake coat upon his back
A ribboned scarf of winter wind
This is the way I picture him.
Delicate lace, painted with care,
Jack Frost leaves his gift
For all to share.

Christmas Is Love

Christmas is love
Around a fir tree
Christmas is peace
With a star to see.
Christmas is joy
In a friendly heart
Found at year's end
To give the New Year a start.

Dreams

Take your dreams this Christmas
And decorate the tree.
Look up high
And once again
The glowing star you'll see.
Take your dreams
And carry them
Into the coming year.
Dreams are made of hope and love
Whenever faith is near.

To Have You Beside Me

To have you beside me
At the end of day,
As we watch the children
Laugh and play,
These are the moments
I treasure each year,
As Christmas draws nigh
With the family near.

Jessica

Jessica was barely three
As we stood there together
And looked at the tree.
But just for that moment
Before my eyes
Was this little miracle
Of a lovable size.
Jessica was barely three
As we stood there together
And looked at the tree.

Christmas Cloud

Christmas cloud, a jollyman
High up in the sky,
All summer long looked for shade
As other clouds passed by.
He must keep cool to make the snow
When winter rolled around.
So he rested in the shade
When'ere it could be found.
When autumn leaves began to fall
This was his busiest time of all.

One night he felt the cold, cold wind
It blew and blew and blew.
All the little children
Felt the cold wind too.
Skates and skis would soon come out
From closets down below;
Shovels would be dancing
Up and down the walks in snow.

As neighbors shared their greetings
In merry Christmas talk,
Christmas cloud was busy
Letting snowflakes drop.
A beautiful sight to see
This winter world of snow;
On every graceful green fir tree
Christmas lights began to glow.

Christmas cloud heard voices
All across the town:
Merry, merry Christmas
Greeted snowflakes falling down.
Along with Christmas greetings
He heard them once again
Wishing friend and neighbor
Peace on earth—good will to men.

Easter Prayer

Easter brings a miracle
Of special little things,
Violets of purple
Butterflies with wings,
Lillies with their petals white
Bird songs fill the air,
Blend into a miracle
To make an Easter prayer.

The Violet

Blushing pink, a violet
Looked out the windowpane.
And laughed to see the snowflakes
As winter howled again.

Her color like a blushing bride
Spread over velvet leaves of green.
Displayed to winter snow outside
What being warm inside could mean.

Seasons

In spring I heard the April rain
Bring love to violets once again.
Red roses in the month of June
Gave love in every blushing bloom.
October leaves of red and gold
Spread love both near and far.
Then came the love of winter
In a bright December star.

This Is the Tree

This is the tree
For the family this year.
The lights are lit.
And the presents are near.
At the very top
Is a bright gold star,
To spread our love,
Both near and far.
This is the tree
For the family this year,
How very special
To have them so near,
To be together
At Christmas time,
Is a treasured gift
That I can call mine.

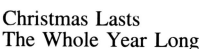

Christmas Lasts
The Whole Year Long

Christmas lasts the whole year long
In green fir tree and robin song.
Snow white clouds high overhead
Raindrops for the violet bed.
Fishes swimming in rippling stream,
Reflect another Christmas dream.
So when I walk in summer's glow,
I'll look at roses and I'll know
That Christmas lasts the whole year long
In April rain and summer's song.

Special Things for Christmas

Special things for Christmas.
Boughs from the green fir tree,
Berries so red from the holly
And a lot of love from me.
Songs from the birds flying by,
Light from the stars in the sky,
Walking together in the winter cold
With only each other's hand to hold.
Special things for Christmas,
Treasures we understand,
For the years we've been together
As a woman and a man.

Jewels of Love

The song of the cardinal
On a cold winter day,
Blends with the holly berry
Red in its glow.
Jewels of love
In the winter snow.

84

Who Says There Isn't Magic

Who says there isn't magic?
I found it one bright day,
High up on a hill top
Where children laugh and play.

The trees were rocking to and fro
In winds so fancy free,
And one I trimmed with tinsel
And I called it Christmas tree.

The children with their bright red sleds
Were laughing with delight,
But one could hear the silence
When I pinned the star so bright.

And then their laughter in the wind
Was carried far and wide,
And I felt the Christmas magic
Sweep across the country side.

Unaware

We sat around the table,
Love was always there.
We didn't even notice,
The gray streaks in her hair.
Her busy hands were making,
Sweet cakes for oven baking,
And on her face were wrinkles,
But we were unaware.
For sunshine filled the laughing room,
We didn't even know,
That love and sunshine disappear
When mothers have to go.

There's Never a Question Why

When Christmas has gathered the family
With mother there in her chair,
And grand-daughter is wearing blue ribbons
Of velvet bows in her hair,
Dad is already waiting
To pass out the presents once more,
And daughter is once again sitting
In her favorite place on the floor,
Son wears his bright red sweater,
And grandson has on his bow tie,
Christmas has gathered the family,
And there's never a question why.

The Little Bear

Oh, I remember the little bear
Dozing and dreaming in the livingroom
    chair,
Waiting for Santa to come in his sleigh
To bring him some honey for Christmas
    day.
Resting his chin on his tiny paws
His head held visions of Santa Claus.
All year long he had been very good
In just the way that little bears should.
Now, Santa had heard of the little bear
Dozing and dreaming in the livingroom
    chair.
So, in his sleigh he put that nite
A jar of honey with ribbons bright.
On the tag he wrote with care
From Santa Claus to my favorite bear.

Joys of Christmas

All the joys of Christmas
To share in just one day,
The secrets of a gift,
The children there in play,
The fireside with its glow of warmth
The decorated tree,
All the happy faces
What a joyous sight to see.
The music of the carols sung
In candlelight so fair,
All the joys of Christmas
That a family can share.

The Little Fir Tree

I'm lonesome to-nite the little tree said.
On my branches there are no ribbons of red.
No presents below—nary a one,
So I say to myself, Why have you come?
I knew I should tell this little tree,
Just what this nite could really be.
So with my voice, I gave this reply,
You have all the light from the stars in the sky.
Your branches are a haven for the animals here
Not just to-nite, but all thru the year.
The snowflakes falling, in their winter design
Blanket your branches, at Christmas time.
And the colors of birds who stop here to rest,
Why all of your colors, are the very best.
The whistling wind carols to you
With songs that are always very new.
You welcome the dawn in sunshine bright,
And the moon and the stars bid you good-night.
The clouds are your sails in the heavenly sea,
And the rain that they give, makes you grow little tree.
And high on this hill, where only you,
Have such a wonderful, wonderful view
Of the church in the valley down there below
With the tall, tall steeple that's as white as the snow
Where the chime of the church bells is starting to ring
Sending love to our Savior, the heavenly king.
How can you be lonesome, with so much—to see?
I guess I'm not, said the little fir tree.

A Carol of Christmas

Sing me a carol of Christmas
Saying a little prayer
Children's voices, older voices,
Echoing in the air.
Sing me a carol of Christmas
Of a manger and wise men three
Wrap it all as a present
And put it under the tree.

It's Christmas

It's Christmas!
The tree is trimmed
Lights are blinking off and on
Children's eyes are closed in sleep
Awaiting Christmas morn.

It's Christmas!
There's magic everywhere
Bells are ringing
People singing
Snowflakes fill the air.

It's Christmas!
The little star
Is spreading rays of light
To bring both peace and love
To all this Christmas night.

My Christmas Wish

My Christmas wish
Old fashion 'tis true
But this is the gift
I give only to you.

Remember this day
As the new year begins
Remember the love
From the bell
As it rings;
Each day
Count your blessings
That all
Come so free;
Remember my love
Remember me.
As you
Look at the star
So high above,
Give thanks
For His blessings,
Give thanks
For His Love.

This is my wish
Old fashion 'tis true
But this is the gift
I give only to you.

Just Like Little Girls Do

In her little fur muff
And her tiny gold locket
She was just like a child
I once knew;
She skipped
And she hopped
And she laughed
When she walked,
Just like little girls do.

The little gold locket
Swung on the chain
And her hands
Were cozy and warm,
And I thought of the blessings
That Christmas day
When a new granddaughter was born.

Christmas Love

The happy years when she was small
And thought the Christmas tree was tall
Her eyes would sparkle and look around
Where Christmas surprises could be found;
She ran and scampered all about
And laughed with childhood grace
And I was happy to see once more
Christmas love on my granddaughter's face.

Busy Hands

Christmas is for children
No matter what you say
Such thoughts ran through a mother's mind
As she gave her time away;
The hours went by with busy hands
She thought of the star above
For Christmas was a happy time
When gifts were made with love.

Christmas Welcome

I'll give you a Christmas
To remember well
Here is a chime
From a silver bell

A ribbon of red
To make a bright bow
And a Christmas star
With a heavenly glow

A green fir tree
So straight and tall
In a room filled with laughter
From children so small

A snowflake or two
Of sparkling white
And an angel to bless you
On Christmas night

A wreath on the door
To welcome your friends
And a year filled with happiness
That never ends.

Christmas Wish

One Christmas wish for all tonight
One Christmas wish from the star so bright
One Christmas wish that has no end
Of peace on earth—good will to men.

Glowing Star

Oh Christmas tree with glowing star
Lift high our hopes today
Give us the power to live and love
A bit of Christmas everyday.

Star's Light

So many things get broken
So many things grow old
But always the light
From the little star
Is just as bright as gold.

Christmas Spirit

There is something about Christmas
When the snow is on the ground
That we remember friends nearby
And others out of town.
Why can't the Christmas spirit
Last the whole year through?
Why do we as the old year ends
Vow to do better in the new?

The Little Tree

The little tree listened
And heard our prayer
To let friends know
That we really care
Not just at Christmas
But the whole year through
And the tree spread its branches
And our love grew and grew.

Daffodil

A little star looked down below,
A bit of stardust touched the snow,
And in the spring the garden found
A daffodil above the ground.

Gratitude

In Gratitude
I bow my head,
With peaceful thoughts
My daily bread.

Stars

Stars are the candles of the night.

Christmas Wreath

The maple tree wore autumn red,
The fir tree dressed in green;
Made Christmas seem a wreath away
With ribbons in between.

The Poet's Hour

Inspiration, then paper and pen,
Record the thoughts of poets when
They see before their eyes,
A bit of life pass quickly by.
A bird, a tree, a sunset bright,
A table lit by candlelight,
A song, a smile, a young child's face,
Hands joined 'neath chin, lips saying grace,
A church with clock on highest tower,
Become a verse in the poet's hour.

Amanda

Amanda is a little girl
Who hugs her teddy bear.
She talks to him all thru the day
And tells him secrets they can share.
Amanda loves her teddy bear
And shows him to her friends.
She always keeps him close nearby
And when the daytime ends,
She quickly climbs the flight of stairs
And all the while she sings
The songs that make a teddy bear
The greatest of all kings.
Before she crawls into her bed
She kneels there on the floor
And Teddy says his prayers with her
Like so many times before.
So off to dreamland once again
Amanda and her friend
Will hold each other tight in sleep
With blessings and amen.

Bless the children in their beds,
And leave your love beside their sleds.

Almost Ten

The world of a child was on display
On the big toy counter in the store that day.
And a mother stood looking at the special toys
That delighted the hearts of growing boys:
The bag of brightly colored blocks she had bought when he was
     one,
And the red and white bouncing ball that had given him such fun.
Then the brown stuffed teddy when he became two,
With the big base drum trimmed with bright, bright blue.
The pretty colored picture books for his big brown eyes to see,
She had put among his other gifts when he was barely three.
And the little wind-up trucks he'd played with on the floor
Had been his prized possessions the year that he turned four.
There were cowboy hats and shirts and guns and soldiers oh so
     bold—
These were the gifts he had received when he was five years old.
Six whole years had sped away, and when she shopped in the
     store that day
Tiny records had been her choice to blend their music with her
     child's voice.
When he was seven, erector sets became his favorite play—
New shapes took place around his room when school let out that
     day.
And then when he was finally eight and now was fairly tall
His only love and interest was for the game of ball.
The baseball mitt had found its space with older much used toys,
And in the game he took his base with all the neighbor boys.
Last year had seen the passing time give way to birthday number
     nine,
And in the world of books he found the world that had been
     proven round.
The mother, who was standing there, slowly turned, and then,
Wondered what a mother bought—when her son was almost ten.

The Little Church

The little church still stands,
In the small New England town;
And the steeple white,
Is lit with light;
And Christmas is all around.

Ribbons in the Sky

Christmas ribbons in the sky
Bright red cardinals flying by.
Singing carols of Christmas cheer
Heralding the bright new year.

Ribbons Red

Ribbons red—ribbons red
I'm wrapping each gift with care,
Ribbons red—ribbons red
I'll save one to tie in your hair.

Winter Shawl

A pattern of lace in each snowflake,
Only God knows the design;
Making a shawl in December,
To last thru the wintertime.

Ribbons

Ribbons are for love she said
And gave me one of Christmas red.

Trim the Tree

This year we'll trim the tree again
And wrap each gift with care
And tuck in just a little love
For all of you to share.

Santa's Dream

Santa's dream for Christmas
For every face a smile,
Pockets filled with laughter
To give to every child.

Merry, merry Christmas
Echoes from the snow,
Peace lights every window
With candles all aglow.

Santa's dream for Christmas
The star so high above
Will welcome in the new year,
Fill every home with LOVE.

Christmas Memories

Up the stair and down the stair
There were toys everywhere.
Children's laughter filled the hall
When all the children were so small.
Now in the glow of Christmas light
Childhood memories fill the night.
There is no laughter in the hall
No toys upon the stair,
But there are memories in our hearts
With children's laughter everywhere.

Thank You God

Thank you God for giving me
Another year to trim the tree.

Holiday Greetings

Our hearts are lighter on this day
Because we're giving love away.
Holiday greetings fill the air
With love for all the children there.

A Little Candle

A little candle
With flame so bright
Was placed on a table
One Christmas night;
Give warmth and love
With your little flame
This is our wish
In His sacred name.

Friendship

Christmas is loving
Giving and then
Caring and calling
Remembering a friend.

Oh what joy the cards can bring
Friends are brought closer in remembering.

Gifts

When hearts hold love to give away,
Joy fills each home on Christmas day.

Christmas is wrapping each gift with care,
Bowing your head and saying a prayer.

Fir Trees

Fir trees dressed in forest green
Candles show their flame. . . .
Stars light up the heaven above
Where angels call His name.

Christmas

Christmas is a holy ground,
Where stars give light,
And bells resound.

The Story

With your arms around the children
Tell the story once again
Of the Savior, of His coming,
Bringing peace good will to men.

No Matter What . . .

No matter what may change
Christmas never will.
The star will still glow bright;
There will be pine upon the hill.

No matter what may change
Christmas will remain the same.
We will bow our heads in prayer
And repeat His sacred name.

A Wish for You

Green trees candles bright
Peace be with you
On Christmas night.

Candlelight

Christmas memories fill the night,
Woven into candlelight.

Christmas Is Over

They say that Christmas is over,
The tree is down;
The colored lights have gone out
All over town.
The red ribboned wreaths
Have left every door
And no rushing crowd
Fills every store;
But if you look high
On a cold winter night,
You can still see the star
Shining so bright.

Prayer

The prayer for Peace
Each day we live,
Is the greatest gift
That one can give.

Don't Forget

Time to take the tree down and put
        the things away;
But don't forget to keep quite near
The LOVE you'll give thru out the year.

About the Author

Cynthia Holt Cummings, born in West Boylston, Massachusetts, served 33 months during WWII in North Africa and Italy as an Army nurse with the Massachusetts General Hospital reserve unit-6th General. Since 1948 she has lived as a homemaker with her husband in the Birmingham, Michigan area where their son, his wife and their four children also reside. In 1979 Cynthia's early Christmas verse was consolidated and printed as that year's holiday greeting card. Accepting her husband's challenge seven other poetry books, including three teddy bear stories, have since been published.

About the Illustrator

The son of a noted illustrator, Fritz Henning grew up in the environs of an art studio and upon graduation from New York Maritime College, served as a ship's officer for a number of years before becoming a professional artist. Long associated with North Light Publications and with the Famous Artists School, Henning has been constantly involved in the world of visual art, including illustration, painting, designing, teaching and writing about the way of art and artists. Recently retired to New Hampton, New Hampshire, the artist and his wife Jane have four children and 13 grandchildren.